STEP-BY-STEP

Cooking for Christmas

STEP-BY-STEP

Cooking for Christmas

SUE ASHWORTH

•PARRAGON•

First published in Great Britain in 1994 by
Parragon Book Service Ltd
Unit 13–17
Avonbridge Trading Estate
Atlantic Road
Avonmouth
Bristol BS11 9QD

ISBN 0 75250 153 4

Produced by Haldane Mason, London
Printed in Italy

Acknowledgements

Art Direction: Ron Samuels
Editor: Alison Leach
Series Design: Pedro & Frances Prá-Lopez/Kingfisher Design
Page Design : F14 Creative Consultants Ltd
Photography: Joff Lee
Styling: John Lee Studios
Home Economist: Sue Ashworth
Assistant Home Economist: Yvonne Melville

Photographs on pages 6, 20, 34, 46 and 62 reproduced by permission of
ZEFA Picture Library (UK) Ltd.

Note

Tablespoons are assumed to be 15ml. Unless otherwise stated, milk is assumed to be full-fat, eggs are standard size 2 and pepper is freshly ground black pepper.

Contents

✱

CHAPTER ONE

Christmas Baking

❈

Getting ready for Christmas is all part of the fun, although of course it can be quite demanding too. It all seems to happen so quickly – one minute it's the beginning of October, and the next Christmas is almost upon us! So this year, make sure that at least some of the Christmas baking is done. You will feel virtuous because you are so well-prepared, and you will be able to cross a few things off your list so that you can concentrate on other necessities.

Often, the recipes that we cook for Christmas are made just once a year, and only the most confident cooks breeze through all their favourite dishes without having to consult a cookery book. Most of us prefer to check procedures first, and with the recipes in this chapter, you will find that the step-by-step format guides you through each stage, explaining any tricky techniques in both words and pictures. Ingredients for Christmas cookery can be quite expensive too, so we want to make sure that the results are well worth it, in terms of the care and attention we have put in, as well as the money.

You can feel reassured that your efforts will be rewarded if you follow the recipes here. And when you cut the Christmas cake or hand round the mince pies, you can enjoy all the compliments that will follow!

Opposite: *The warm glow of Christmas-tree lights provides a welcome invitation into this small German church.*

STEP 1

STEP 3

STEP 4

STEP 5

TRADITIONAL CHRISTMAS CAKE

This delicious Christmas cake is packed with dried fruits and laced with a good tot of rum. Soaking the dried fruit for 2 days in the orange juice and rum plumps it up, making the cake more moist and mature-tasting, but if you haven't much time, just soak the fruit for a few hours.

MAKES ONE 18 CM/7 IN SQUARE OR
20 CM/8 IN ROUND CAKE

finely grated rind of 1 orange
2 tbsp orange juice
500 g/1 lb seedless raisins
250 g/8 oz sultanas
250 g/8 oz currants
60 g/2 oz dates, stoned and chopped
175 g/6 oz glacé cherries, halved
150 ml/¼ pint dark rum
250 g/8 oz molasses sugar
250 g/8 oz butter
4 eggs, beaten
250 g/8 oz plain flour
pinch of salt
1 tsp ground mixed spice
1 tsp ground cinnamon
½ tsp ground nutmeg
60 g/2 oz ground hazelnuts or almonds
30 g/1 oz chopped hazelnuts or almonds

TO DECORATE:
3 tbsp apricot jam
glacé fruits
whole, shelled nuts

1 Put the orange rind and juice, raisins, sultanas, currants, dates, glacé cherries and rum into a large bowl. Stir well, then cover and leave in a cool place for 1–2 days, stirring occasionally.

2 Line an 18 cm/7 in square or 20 cm/8 in round cake tin with double-thickness greaseproof paper.

3 Cream the sugar and butter together until fluffy, and then beat in the eggs gradually. Sift the flour, salt and spices together and fold into the mixture. Add the ground and chopped nuts and the soaked fruit mixture. Stir together gently until well-mixed, and then transfer to the prepared tin, levelling the surface.

4 Bake in a preheated oven at 150°C/ 300°F/Gas Mark 2 for 2–2½ hours, or until a fine skewer inserted into the centre comes out clean. To prevent the top from getting too brown, cover with a piece of brown paper after 1½ hours. Leave to cool completely in the tin.

5 To decorate, warm the apricot jam, rub it through a sieve and brush over the surface of the cake. Arrange the glacé fruits and nuts over the top in an attractive pattern. Brush the fruits and nuts with apricot jam to glaze.

STEP 1: Almond Paste

STEP 2: Almond Paste

STEP 1: Fondant Icing

STEP 2: Fondant Icing

ALMOND PASTE & FONDANT ICING

Almond paste and fondant icing – or sugarpaste – are so easy to make at home, you'll wonder why you ever bought them ready-made. Fondant icing gives a softer finish than Royal Icing (see page 76) and is ideal for colouring and moulding into shapes for decorating the Christmas cake.

ALMOND PASTE

MAKES ABOUT 750 G/1½ LB
COVERS ONE 18 CM/7 IN SQUARE OR
  20 CM/8 IN ROUND CAKE

350 g/12 oz ground almonds
175 g/6 oz caster sugar
175 g/6 oz icing sugar
1 tsp lemon juice
3–4 drops almond flavouring
2 egg whites from small eggs, beaten lightly
icing sugar for dusting
warmed, sieved apricot jam

1 Put the ground almonds and caster sugar into a large bowl. Sift in the icing sugar, using a non-metallic sieve. Stir well, and then add the lemon juice, almond essence and lightly beaten egg white. Mix to form a soft but firm paste.

2 Turn the paste on to a work surface dusted with icing sugar and knead lightly until smooth; avoid overhandling or it could become oily. Place in a polythene bag and seal until required.

3 Brush the surface of the cake with warmed, sieved apricot jam before putting on the almond paste.

FONDANT ICING

MAKES ABOUT 800 G/1 LB 10 OZ
COVERS ONE 18 CM/7 IN SQUARE OR
  20 CM/8 IN ROUND CAKE

750 g/1½ lb icing sugar
1 egg white from a large egg
3 tbsp liquid glucose
icing sugar for dusting

1 Sift the icing sugar into a large bowl, using a non-metallic sieve. Whisk the egg white lightly and mix with the liquid glucose. Add to the sugar, beating with a wooden spoon to mix. Gather together to form a ball.

2 Transfer to a work surface, dusted with icing sugar, and knead until smooth and pliable. If the icing is too soft, add a little extra sifted icing sugar. Store in a sealed polythene bag, making sure that all the air is excluded.

3 To ice a cake, roll out icing on a surface dusted with icing sugar. Lift on to the cake and smooth it down with your hands, also dusted with icing sugar.

4 Colour fondant icing with paste food colourings and cut into holly leaves and berries to decorate.

STEP 1

STEP 2

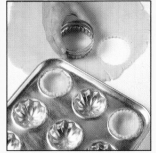

STEP 3

STEP 4

FESTIVE MINCE PIES

These mince pies are made with a crumbly, rich shortcrust pastry. Fill them with your homemade Rum & Raisin Mincemeat and top with a spoonful of whipped cream, thick-set yogurt or brandy butter. Serve them warm for a heavenly treat!

MAKES ABOUT 20

350 g/12 oz plain flour
pinch of salt
175 g/6 oz butter, chilled
45 g/1½ oz caster sugar
3 egg yolks, beaten
1–2 tbsp chilled water
500 g/1 lb Rum & Raisin Mincemeat (see page 36)
lightly beaten egg white
icing sugar for dredging

1 Sift the flour and salt into a large bowl. Cut the butter into pieces and then add to the flour. Rub in the butter using your fingertips, until the mixture resembles fine breadcrumbs.

2 Add the caster sugar to the flour mixture. Mix the egg yolks with 1 tbsp of the chilled water. Make a well in the centre of the flour mixture and add the egg yolks, stirring with a round-bladed knife to make a soft dough. Add a little extra chilled water if the dough is too dry.

3 Knead the dough lightly until smooth, and then roll out two-thirds of it thinly on a lightly floured surface. Using a 7.5 cm/3 in biscuit cutter, stamp out 18–20 rounds and use to line patty tins.

4 Spoon the mincemeat into the patty tins, to come about half-way up the sides. Roll out the remaining pastry and use Christmas biscuit cutters to cut out shapes, such as stars, bells and trees. Position on top of the mince pies and brush with lightly beaten egg white.

5 Bake in a preheated oven at 220°C/425°F/Gas Mark 7 for 15–20 minutes, or until light golden brown. Leave to cool slightly, and then remove from the tins. Transfer to a wire rack and leave to cool until they are not too hot to handle comfortably. Serve while still warm, sprinkled with icing sugar.

FREEZING

Homemade mince pies are ideal for freezing, so you can make plenty in advance. Freeze them 'open' on a tray, then pack them into plastic bags and label the bags with the date. Once defrosted, warm them for 10 minutes in a low oven before serving.

STOLLEN

Stollen is a sweet, fruity German Christmas bread, enriched with butter and eggs, and this version has a hidden filling of almond paste. Dredged with lots of icing sugar, it makes a delicious alternative to the traditional Christmas Cake.

STEP 1

STEP 2

STEP 3

STEP 4

MAKES 2

60 g/2 oz glacé cherries
60 g/2 oz sultanas
60 g/2 oz seedless raisins
30 g/1 oz angelica, chopped
30 g/1 oz candied peel, chopped finely
6 tbsp rum
1 kg/2 lb plain flour
$^{1}/_{2}$ tsp salt
1 sachet (8 g) easy-blend yeast
125 g/4 oz caster sugar
$^{1}/_{2}$ tsp ground mace
1 tsp finely grated lemon rind
300 ml/$^{1}/_{2}$ pint milk
2 eggs, beaten
125 g/4 oz butter, melted
60 g/2 oz flaked almonds
350 g/12 oz Almond Paste (see page 10)
icing sugar for dredging

1 Put the glacé cherries, sultanas, raisins, angelica and candied peel into a bowl. Add the rum and leave to soak overnight.

2 Sift the flour and salt into a large bowl and stir in the easy-blend yeast. Stir in the sugar, mace and lemon rind. Heat the milk until it is lukewarm, and then add to the beaten eggs with the melted butter, stirring well. Make a well in the centre of the flour and add the milk mixture, stirring to combine.

3 Gather the dough together and knead on a floured work surface until smooth and elastic, about 10–15 minutes. Drain the soaked fruit well and pat dry with paper towels. Press into the dough with the flaked almonds and knead lightly to incorporate it, but avoid overhandling or the dough could become discoloured. Keep your hands lightly floured to make it more manageable. Place in a large greased bowl, cover and leave to rise in a warm place until doubled in size, about 2 hours.

4 Knock back the dough and knead lightly until smooth. Divide into 2 equal parts. Roll each piece into a strip about 30 x 20 cm/12 x 8 in. Divide the almond paste into 2 pieces and roll into sausage shapes about 25 cm/10 in long. Lay on the dough, fold over and seal. Transfer to greased baking sheets and leave to rise until doubled in size.

5 Bake the loaves in a preheated oven at 190°C/375°F/Gas Mark 5 for about 30–35 minutes, until golden brown. Leave to cool on a wire rack and then dredge with plenty of icing sugar.

STEP 2

STEP 3

STEP 3

STEP 5

CHOCOLATE YULE LOG

This is a sophisticated version of a chocolate log, flavoured with brandy and filled with a mixture of fresh cream and chestnut purée.

MAKES ONE 23 CM/9 IN LOG

few drops of vegetable oil
125 g/4 oz caster sugar, plus extra 2 tsp
4 eggs
60 g/ 2 oz plain flour
30 g/ 1 oz cocoa powder

FILLING:
90 ml/ 3 fl oz double (thick) cream
60 g/2 oz sweetened chestnut purée
2 tbsp brandy

CHOCOLATE BUTTER CREAM:
90 g/ 3 oz caster sugar
4 tbsp water
2 egg yolks
125 g/4 oz unsalted butter, softened
125 g/4 oz icing sugar, sifted
60 g/ 2 oz plain (dark) chocolate, melted

1 Grease and line a 33 x 23 cm/13 x 9 in Swiss (jelly) roll tin with a little oil and non-stick greaseproof paper. Cut a second piece of greaseproof paper a little larger than the tin and sprinkle with 2 tsp sugar. Set aside.

2 Whisk the sugar and eggs in a large bowl until very pale and light, using a hand-held electric mixer or a wire whisk.

3 Sift the flour and cocoa powder together. Fold into the egg mixture gently. Pour into the prepared tin, level the surface and bake in a preheated oven at 220°C/ 425°F/Gas Mark 7 for 7–9 minutes until firm, yet springy to the touch. Turn out on to the sugared paper. Peel away the lining paper and trim the edges. Cover with a damp tea towel and leave to cool completely.

4 To make the filling, whip the cream until thick and stir in the chestnut purée. Sprinkle the brandy over the cake. Spread the cream mixture over the sponge and roll up from one long edge.

5 To make the chocolate butter cream, heat the sugar and water gently until the sugar dissolves, then boil rapidly until syrupy. Whisk the egg yolks, adding the sugar syrup in a steady stream, until the mixture becomes thick and pale. Add the butter and the cooled, melted chocolate. Beat in the icing sugar.

6 Cut a 7.5 cm/3 in slice from the chocolate roll and cut in half diagonally. Attach to the sides of the roll with some butter cream. Cover the log with the remaining butter cream and use a skewer or fork to make a bark pattern.

STEP 1

STEP 3

STEP 4

STEP 5

SPICED FRUIT GARLAND

There is nothing like the delicious smell of yeast cooking for creating a warm, homely atmosphere. It must be something to do with the anticipation of good things to eat! This wonderful Spiced Fruit Garland certainly lives up to expectations.

SERVES 12

425 g/ 14 oz strong plain (bread) flour
1/2 tsp salt
60 g/2 oz butter
60 g/2 oz caster sugar
1 sachet (8 g) easy-blend yeast
180 ml/6 fl oz warm milk
1 egg, beaten

FILLING:
150 g/5 oz mixed dried fruit
30 g/1 oz glacé cherries, chopped
60 g/2 oz ground almonds
60 g/2 oz light muscovado sugar
1 tsp ground cinnamon
1/2 tsp ground nutmeg
30 g/1 oz butter, melted

TO DECORATE:
60 g/2 oz icing sugar
glacé cherries
chopped nuts
angelica

1 Sift the flour and salt together in a large bowl. Rub in the butter and then stir in the sugar and easy-blend yeast. Make a well in the centre and add the warm milk and beaten egg. Draw the flour into the egg and milk gradually, mixing well to make a smooth dough.

2 Knead the dough on a lightly floured work surface for 8–10 minutes. Place in a lightly oiled bowl and cover with a cloth. Stand in a warm place and leave to rise until doubled in size.

3 Knead lightly for 1 minute, and then roll out into a 40 x 23 cm/ 16 x 9 in rectangle. Mix together all the filling ingredients and spread over the rectangle, leaving a 2 cm/¾ in border around the edge. From the long edge, roll the rectangle into a cylinder, pressing the edge to seal it. Form the roll into a circle, sealing the ends together.

4 Lift the ring on to a greased baking sheet and then cut it into 12 slices at about 5 cm/2 in intervals, without cutting right through, keeping the circular shape. Twist each slice so that a cut surface lies uppermost. Leave in a warm place for 30–40 minutes to rise.

5 Bake in a preheated oven at 200°C/ 400°F/Gas Mark 6 for 25–30 minutes until risen and golden brown. Cool on a wire rack. Mix the icing sugar with a little water to make a thin glacé icing and drizzle over. Arrange the glacé cherries on top, and sprinkle with the chopped nuts and angelica.

CHAPTER TWO

Festive Sweets & Biscuits

❋

Sweets and treats are so nice to have around at Christmas – it's all part of that feeling that we want to let ourselves go a little, and submit to a small helping of over-indulgence.

In this section, you'll find some delicious ideas for fulfilling the desire to make and eat a few sweet things. What's more, the recipes are perfect to give away as presents with that homemade touch – ideal for children to give to aunts and grannies. Get their help in making some of these treats – it will give them something constructive to do in those exciting few days just before Christmas. Some of the ideas can be used as tree decorations too, so the kids can see their efforts displayed in pride of place – but don't expect them to stay on the tree too long; little fingers will soon be unwrapping them!

If you plan to give these goodies for gifts, remember that presentation is everything. Spend a little time and effort on packaging the sweets and biscuits prettily, in attractive Christmas boxes, or wrap them individually and tie with ribbon. Friends and relations will be delighted with their presents, and even more impressed when they taste them.

Opposite: Candy sticks like these make bright, colourful Christmas decorations when wrapped and tied with ribbon.

APPLE & MINCEMEAT SQUARES

*A deliciously fruity combination of apples and mincemeat is spiced
with cinnamon and sandwiched between a crumbly, melt-in-the-mouth
cake mixture in this easy-to-make recipe.*

STEP 2

STEP 3

STEP 4

STEP 5

MAKES ABOUT **12** SQUARES

250 g/8 oz butter
250 g/8 oz light muscovado sugar
500 g/1 lb self-raising flour
pinch of salt
1 large (size 1) or 2 small (size 3) eggs
500 g/1 lb cooking apples
finely grated rind of 1 lemon
2 tbsp lemon juice
4 tbsp mincemeat
60 g/2 oz demerara sugar
1 tsp ground cinnamon
30 g/1 oz coarse porridge oats
icing sugar for dredging

1 Put the butter into a saucepan and heat gently until melted. Add the muscovado sugar, stir thoroughly and leave to cool slightly.

2 Sift the flour and salt into a large bowl and make a well in the centre. Add the melted butter mixture. Beat the eggs and add to the mixture, stirring well to combine thoroughly.

3 Transfer two–thirds of the mixture to a greased and lined 30 x 25 cm/ 12 x 10 in shallow cake tin, pressing down well.

4 Peel and slice the apples thinly, and place in a bowl with the lemon rind and juice. (The juice helps to prevent the apples from turning brown.) Add the mincemeat, demerara sugar and cinnamon, stirring well to mix. Spoon over the prepared base in an even layer.

5 Mix the porridge oats into the reserved cake mixture and scatter evenly over the fruit.

6 Bake in a preheated oven at 190°C/ 375°F/Gas Mark 5 for about 35–40 minutes.

7 When cool, cut into squares and remove from the cake tin. Dredge with icing sugar before serving.

PUDDING MIXTURE

While this is really a cake mixture, it also doubles as a delicious pudding served hot with a jug of custard sauce. Halve the quantity to serve 6 people.

STEP 1

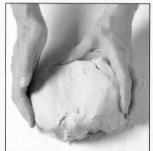

STEP 2

STEP 3

STEP 5

CHRISTMAS SHORTBREAD

Make this wonderful shortbread and then give it the Christmas touch by cutting it into shapes with seasonal biscuit cutters – bells, stars, angels or Christmas trees. If you like, you can even hang the biscuits from the tree, but don't expect them to stay there for too long!

MAKES ABOUT **24**

125 g/4 oz caster sugar
250 g/8 oz butter
350 g/12 oz plain flour, sifted
pinch of salt

To decorate:
60 g/2 oz icing sugar
silver balls
glacé cherries
angelica

1 Beat the sugar and butter together in a large bowl until combined (thorough creaming is not necessary).

2 Sift in the flour and salt and work together to form a stiff dough. Turn out on to a lightly floured surface. Knead lightly for a few moments until smooth, but avoid overhandling. Chill for 10–15 minutes.

3 Roll out the dough on a lightly floured work surface and cut into shapes with Christmas cutters. Place on greased baking sheets.

4 Bake the biscuits in a preheated oven at 180°C/350°F/Gas Mark 4 for 10–15 minutes until pale golden brown. Leave on the baking sheets to cool for 10 minutes, then transfer to a wire rack to cool completely.

5 Mix the icing sugar with a little water to make a glacé icing, and use to ice the biscuits. Decorate with silver balls, tiny pieces of glacé cherries and angelica. Store in an airtight tin.

EASY ICING

Small tubes of brightly coloured 'writing icing' can be bought from supermarkets or cake-decorating shops. They are very handy to use for decorating these biscuits.

READY FOR THE TREE

If you want to use these biscuits to decorate the Christmas tree, wrap them in cellophane and tie them with narrow ribbon or coloured string. If you prefer, make larger biscuits, wrap in cellophane and tie with tartan ribbon to give as gifts.

STEP 1

STEP 2

STEP 3

STEP 4

APRICOT BRANDY TRUFFLES

*Homemade truffles are easy to make and a treat to eat. Pack them into
small attractive boxes to make a perfect gift with the personal touch.*

MAKES ABOUT 20

175 g/6 oz plain (dark) chocolate
60 g/2 oz dark muscovado sugar
30 g/1 oz butter
2 egg yolks
1 tbsp apricot brandy
1 tbsp milk
30 g/1 oz dried apricots, chopped finely
30 g/1 oz cake or biscuit crumbs
*60 g/2 oz chocolate vermicelli or 30 g/1 oz
   cocoa powder*

1 Melt the chocolate in a medium
bowl placed over a pan of gently
simmering water. Add the sugar and
butter, stirring until melted.

2 Stir in the egg yolks, apricot brandy
and milk. Heat gently, stirring
constantly, for 2 minutes.

3 Add the apricots and then mix in
the cake or biscuit crumbs. Beat
the mixture thoroughly and leave to
cool. Then chill until firm enough to
handle.

4 Form the mixture into about 20
balls and roll in chocolate
vermicelli or cocoa powder. Place in
sweet cases and store in a cool place.

5 To pack, wrap the truffles
separately in cellophane, gather
into a pouch and tie with ribbon. Pack
them in attractive gift boxes.

6 Keep the truffles refrigerated and
eat within 2 weeks.

HANDY TIP

Dusting your hands with a little cocoa
powder will help to prevent the mixture
from becoming too sticky when forming it
into balls.

SUBSTITUTES

If you wish, substitute rum or ordinary
brandy for the apricot brandy and use
raisins instead of dried apricots. Drinking
chocolate can also be used instead of
cocoa powder, if you prefer.

CHRISTMAS TREE CLUSTERS

Popcorn is the perfect nibble to have around at Christmas, and makes a pleasant change from crisps and peanuts. If wrapped in cellophane and tied with ribbon, Christmas Tree Clusters make ideal presents or decorations for the Christmas tree.

STEP 1

MAKES ABOUT 16

1 tbsp vegetable oil
30 g/1 oz popcorn kernels (unpopped corn)
30 g/1 oz butter
60 g/2 oz soft light brown sugar
4 tbsp golden syrup
30 g/1 oz glacé cherries, chopped
60 g/2 oz sultanas or raisins
30 g/1 oz ground almonds
15 g/¹/₂ oz nibbed almonds
¹/₂ tsp ground mixed spice

1 To pop the corn, heat the oil in a large saucepan that has a lid, or in a special popcorn pan. The oil is hot enough when a kernel spins around in the pan. Add the popcorn kernels, put on the lid and pop the corn over a medium-high heat, shaking the pan frequently.

2 Remove the pan from the heat and wait until the popping sound subsides.

3 Put the butter, sugar and golden syrup into a large saucepan and heat gently, stirring frequently, to dissolve the sugar. Do not allow the mixture to boil. Remove from the heat once the sugar is dissolved.

4 Add the popped corn, glacé cherries, sultanas or raisins, ground and nibbed almonds, and mixed spice to the syrup mixture, stirring well. Leave to cool for a few minutes.

5 Shape the mixture into small balls. Leave to cool completely, then wrap in cellophane and tie with ribbon.

STEP 2

STEP 4

POPPING CORN

Children will enjoy making some Christmas Tree Clusters. Take care when popping corn – the oil in the pan is very hot and can burn.

PECAN NUT CLUSTERS

Omit the cherries, sultanas, ground almonds and mixed spice and replace with 60 g/2 oz roughly chopped pecan nuts and ¹/₂ tsp ground cinnamon to make Pecan Nut Clusters.

STEP 5

STEP 3

STEP 4

STEP 5

STEP 6

WHITE CHOCOLATE FLORENTINES

These attractive jewelled biscuits are coated with white chocolate to give them a delicious flavour. They have a wonderfully chewy texture and one is never enough, so make sure that you make plenty!

MAKES ABOUT 24

200 g/7 oz butter
250 g/8 oz caster sugar
125 g/4 oz walnuts, chopped
125 g/4 oz almonds, chopped
60 g/2 oz sultanas, chopped
30 g/1 oz glacé cherries, chopped
30 g/1 oz mixed candied peel, chopped finely
2 tbsp single (thin) cream
225 g/8 oz white chocolate

1 Line 3–4 baking sheets with non-stick baking parchment.

2 Melt the butter over a low heat and then add the sugar, stirring until it has dissolved. Boil the mixture for exactly 1 minute. Remove from the heat.

3 Add the walnuts, almonds, sultanas, glacé cherries, candied peel and cream to the saucepan, stirring well to mix.

4 Drop heaped teaspoonfuls of the mixture on to the baking sheets, allowing plenty of room for them to spread while cooking. Bake in a preheated oven at 180°C/350°F/Gas Mark 4 for about 10 minutes, until golden brown.

5 Remove the biscuits from the oven and neaten the edges with a knife while they are still warm. Leave to cool slightly, and then transfer them to a wire rack to cool completely.

6 Melt the chocolate in a bowl placed over a pan of gently simmering water. Spread the underside of the biscuits with chocolate and use a fork to make wavy lines across the surface. Leave to cool completely.

7 Store the Florentines in an airtight tin, kept in a cool place.

MICROWAVE

If you wish, melt the chocolate in a microwave oven. Break the chocolate into pieces, place in a microwaveable bowl and microwave on Full Power for 1½–2 minutes.

TWO COLOURS

A combination of white and plain chocolate Florentines looks very attractive, especially if you are making them as gifts. Pack them in pretty boxes, lined with tissue paper and tied with ribbon.

30

STEP 1

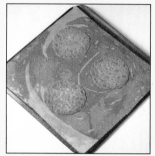

STEP 4

STEP 5

STEP 6

BRANDY SNAP BOATS & BASKETS

These brandy-flavoured biscuits can be rolled into the traditional shape, or formed into baskets to make an ideal container for fresh fruit and cream. The step-by-step photographs show you the tricks of the trade for rolling and shaping them.

MAKES ABOUT 30

125 g/4 oz butter
125 g/4 oz caster sugar
4 tbsp golden syrup
125 g/4 oz plain flour
pinch of salt
1/2 tsp ground ginger
1 tsp brandy

TO DECORATE:
300 ml/1/2 pt double (thick) cream
fresh fruit, such as cape gooseberries, kiwi
   fruit, grapes and nectarines

1 Grease and line 2 baking sheets with non-stick baking parchment. Butter a rolling pin, to be used for shaping the brandy snap boats. Butter the undersides of 3 or 4 clean eggcups, to be used for shaping the baskets.

2 Heat the butter, sugar and syrup gently in a small heavy-based saucepan, until the sugar has melted. (Do not allow the mixture to boil.) Remove from the heat.

3 Sift the flour, salt and ground ginger together, and add to the saucepan with the brandy. Mix well until smooth. Leave to cool slightly.

4 Drop teaspoonfuls of the mixture on to the baking sheets, allowing space for the mixture to spread. Bake in a preheated oven at 180°C/350°F/Gas Mark 4 for 7–10 minutes, until the mixture is golden brown and bubbly, with a lacy texture.

5 Quickly place some of the cooked biscuits over the rolling pin. Arrange some of the biscuits over the eggcups and flute them to form baskets. Leave to cool completely, and then ease them off gently.

6 When ready to serve, whip the cream and fill the brandy snap boats and baskets. Decorate with fresh fruit. Serve soon, so that the biscuits do not become soggy. (Unfilled boats and baskets can be kept in an airtight tin for 7–10 days.)

TOO HARD?

If you find that the cooked biscuits have hardened before you have had a chance to shape them, pop the baking sheet back into the oven for a few moments to soften them again.

CHAPTER THREE

POTTED GOODIES

❋

There's something about making Christmas preserves that gives a lingering sense of satisfaction. It must be something to do with seeing the results of your efforts potted up in attractive jars, instead of watching them disappear the moment they are made. If you're involved in school fêtes, Christmas bazaars or fund-raising events, you'll find these suggestions perfect for the homemade goods stall.

The food in this chapter helps to provide the finishing flourish to your later preparations. Take, for instance, the Rum & Raisin Mincemeat. It has a delicious mellow flavour that improves with age, making the perfect filling for homemade mince pies and the Apple & Mincemeat Squares on page 22. Because it doesn't contain any suet, it is ideal for vegetarians, and its lower fat content makes it more palatable for many people.

Other recipes include Cumberland Sauce and Cranberry & Red Onion Relish, both excellent for serving with the Christmas Lunch or for adding to a Boxing Day spread. There's also a delicious chunky chutney recipe using parsnips and apples, and a fabulous Apricot & Almond Jam which tastes superb spread on to hot toast, crumpets or muffins. The recipes in this section make very attractive gifts for all lovers of good food – and that covers just about everyone!

Opposite: *Fruits, whether in jams, relishes or chutneys, make delicious treats for Christmas.*

STEP 1

STEP 2

STEP 3

STEP 4

RUM & RAISIN MINCEMEAT

This brilliant recipe for homemade mincemeat doesn't use suet, so it is suitable for vegetarians or those on a low-fat diet. It tastes fabulous in mince pies, and can be used in the recipe for Apple & Mincemeat Squares (see page 22).

MAKES ABOUT 1.5 KG/3 LB

500 g/1 lb raisins
250 g/8 oz sultanas
250 g/8 oz currants
125 g/4 oz glacé cherries, halved
150 ml/¼ pint dark rum, brandy or sherry
2 medium dessert (eating) apples, peeled,
*   cored and chopped finely*
2 tsp mixed spice
½ tsp freshly grated nutmeg
125 g/4 oz chopped roast hazelnuts
250 g/8 oz dark muscovado sugar
4 tbsp hot water
60 g/2 oz butter

1 Put the raisins, sultanas, currants, glacé cherries and rum, brandy or sherry into a large bowl. Mix together thoroughly, then cover and leave in a cool place, stirring occasionally, for 12–24 hours.

2 Blanch the chopped apple in boiling water for 2 minutes, and then drain thoroughly.

3 Add the chopped apple to the soaked dried fruit mixture with the mixed spice, nutmeg and hazelnuts, stirring thoroughly.

4 Put the dark muscovado sugar, hot water and butter into a saucepan. Heat very gently, stirring frequently, until the sugar has melted. Add to the fruit mixture and stir well to combine thoroughly.

5 Pack into sterilized jars, seal and label. Decorate the lids with scraps of colourful fabric, butter muslin or greaseproof paper and tie with string.

STERILIZING JARS

To sterilize jars, wash them thoroughly in hot, soapy water, rinse well with hot water and place on a baking sheet. Warm in a preheated oven at 110°C/225°F/Gas Mark ¼ for 10–15 minutes.

CHRISTMAS BAZAARS

This mincemeat recipe is so quick and easy to make that it is ideal for preparing for Christmas bazaars, school fêtes and and other fund-raising events.

APRICOT & ALMOND JAM

Perfect for gifts, this delicious jam is made from dried apricots and whole blanched almonds, which make it look very attractive in the jars.

STEP 1

STEP 2

STEP 3

STEP 4

MAKES ABOUT 5 x 500 G/1 LB JARS

500 g/1 lb dried apricots
1.75 litres/3 pints water
4 tbsp lemon juice
90 g/3 oz blanched almonds
1.5 kg/3 lb granulated sugar

1 Put the apricots into a very large saucepan with the water. Heat until just boiling and then reduce the heat. Simmer gently, uncovered, for about 1 hour until the apricots are soft and tender.

2 Remove the pan from the heat. Add the lemon juice, almonds and sugar, and stir gently until the sugar has dissolved. Return the pan to the heat and simmer gently until setting point is reached.

3 To test for the setting point, put a teaspoonful of jam on to a cold saucer. Leave it to cool for 1 minute and then push the surface of the cooled jam with your fingertip. The surface will wrinkle if the jam has reached setting point. Remove the pan from the heat.

4 Leave the jam to stand for 5 minutes to settle, and then stir to distribute the fruit and almonds. Pot the jam in warmed sterilized jars and seal while hot.

5 Leave to cool completely before labelling. Decorate the lids with scraps of bright fabric or butter muslin and tie with ribbon or string.

DRIED APRICOTS

If using ready-to-eat dried apricots, which contain more moisture, reduce the quantity of water in the recipe to 1.5 litres/2½ pints.

PREVENTING MOULD

Wash the jam jars thoroughly before use, drain them well and then dry them out and warm them in a preheated oven at 110°C/225°F/Gas Mark ¼. Make sure the jam comes up to the rim of the jar, as it will shrink slightly as it cools. Seal the lids while the jam is hot, to keep them free from mould.

STEP 1

STEP 2

STEP 3

STEP 4

CRANBERRY & RED ONION RELISH

This unusual sauce makes a tasty accompaniment to turkey with all the trimmings. Red onions are used in the recipe, but there is no reason why you cannot use ordinary white ones.

MAKES ABOUT 3 X 350 G/12 OZ
JARS

30 g/1 oz butter
2 red onions
grated rind and juice of 1 large orange
500 g/1 lb fresh or frozen cranberries
125 g/4 oz sugar
4 tbsp red wine vinegar
4 tbsp red wine
1/2 tsp ground allspice
pinch of ground cinnamon

1 Slice the red onions thinly.

2 Melt the butter in a medium saucepan and fry the onions gently until softened, about 8–10 minutes.

3 Add the orange rind and juice, and cook gently for 5 minutes.

4 Add the cranberries to the saucepan with the sugar, wine vinegar, red wine and spices. Heat until just boiling and then reduce the heat. Simmer until syrupy, about 15 minutes.

5 Pot the relish in sterilized small glass jars. Place a circle of greaseproof paper over the surface of

each one, and then seal and label the jars. Decorate the lids with fabric or butter muslin and tie with string or ribbon.

ALLSPICE

Allspice is a single spice with the combined flavours of nutmeg, cinnamon and cloves, and it shouldn't be confused with mixed spice.

ALTERNATIVE

If you wish, substitute port or sherry for the red wine.

STORING

Make this relish 2–3 weeks before Christmas if you like. Remember to store it in the refrigerator after opening and use within 2 weeks.

STEP 1

STEP 2

STEP 3

STEP 4

CUMBERLAND SAUCE

A traditional sauce for serving with game birds, Cumberland Sauce is a superb accompaniment to all cold meats. It makes an excellent choice for serving with a Boxing Day spread of cold ham and turkey.

MAKES ABOUT 4 × 250 G/8 OZ JARS

500 g/1 lb redcurrant jelly
450 ml/³/₄ pint port
1 orange
1 lemon
2 tbsp Worcestershire sauce
pinch of cayenne pepper

1 Put the redcurrant jelly into a saucepan and heat gently, stirring to melt it.

2 Add the port to the jelly and heat gently, stirring frequently, until just boiling. Reduce the heat and simmer gently for about 15–20 minutes, or until the sauce has reduced by about one-third. It should be syrupy and quite runny. Leave the sauce to cool.

3 Pare the rind from the orange and lemon, and cut it into fine strips.

4 Squeeze the juice from the fruit. Add to the jelly mixture with the fine strips of rind, the Worcestershire sauce and the cayenne pepper.

5 Pot the sauce in sterilized small glass jars.

6 When cooled, decorate the lids with scraps of bright fabric, butter muslin or greaseproof paper. Tie on with ribbon or string and label the jars.

PARING RIND

The best way to pare the rind thinly from citrus fruit is to use a potato peeler.

HOMEMADE PRESENTS

You can make this sauce at the beginning of December. Once opened, it will keep in the refrigerator for 10–14 days.

Cumberland Sauce makes a tasty gift for anyone who loves good food, so try making plenty of pots to add a homemade touch to your Christmas presents.

STEP 1

STEP 2

STEP 3

STEP 4

PARSNIP, APPLE & GINGER CHUTNEY

Parsnips, being quite sweet, make a chutney with a lovely flavour, especially when combined with apples and fresh root ginger.

MAKES ABOUT 2 KG/4 LB

750 g/1¹/₂ lb parsnips, peeled and chopped
500 g/1 lb cooking apples, peeled, cored and chopped
250 g/8 oz onions, peeled, sliced and chopped
600 ml/1 pint cider vinegar
500 g/1 lb soft brown sugar
2 tsp freshly grated root ginger
¹/₂ tsp ground cloves
1 tsp ground allspice

1 Put the parsnips, apples and onions into a large saucepan with the vinegar. Bring to the boil, then reduce the heat and simmer gently for about 30 minutes, until the onions are tender.

2 Remove the pan from the heat and add the sugar. Stir until it has dissolved.

3 Add the ginger, cloves and allspice. Return to the heat and simmer gently until the mixture is thick and pulpy. (The chutney will thicken only slightly as it cools.)

4 Pot the chutney in warm sterilized jars and seal immediately with vinegar-proof tops.

5 Label when completely cold and decorate the lids with scraps of bright fabric, butter muslin or greaseproof paper, tied on with ribbon or string.

SUGAR

Soft brown sugar is used in this recipe, but you can use ordinary granulated sugar instead, although the colour of the chutney will be slightly paler.

ALTERNATIVE VINEGAR

Ordinary malt vinegar gives a good flavour too, if you want to try an alternative or can't find any cider vinegar.

COLLECTING JARS

Collect attractive jars for potting jams, chutneys and pickles in the months before Christmas – then you won't need to search for them before making this recipe.

CHAPTER FOUR

Christmas Lunch

❀

The anticipation of Christmas lunch is almost as good as the meal itself! Suddenly all the effort of the preceding weeks seems to have been worth it, as everyone settles into the cosy warmth of friends and family.

Having said that, it is so important to get everything just right, so that the meal lives up to expectations. Planning is really what it is all about, and delegation too – for you mustn't expect to do all the preparations yourself, as it's supposed to be a break for you too. Enlist the help of your family, giving them specific jobs to do – even if it's only peeling the potatoes.

This chapter will help you to get organized, and will give you all the information you need to produce perfect results. As well as recipes for turkey with all the trimmings, there is a wonderful chestnut and mushroom dish for vegetarian guests, instructions for the best-ever Rich Christmas Puddings and a light recipe for Frozen Citrus Soufflés, to give a delicious alternative for dessert. You may find that these few pages will become well-thumbed as you refer to them for your Christmas cooking for years to come!

Opposite: *On a cold winter afternoon, the warm glow of a Christmas tree seen through the window is very inviting.*

STEP 1

STEP 2

STEP 3

STEP 4

ROAST TURKEY WITH BACON ROLLS

The centrepiece of the table for Christmas lunch, this golden Roast Turkey takes pride of place. Use small bunches of fresh herbs – such as sage, rosemary, bay leaves and thyme – or fresh watercress to garnish.

SERVES 8–10

5–7 kg/10–14 lb turkey, thoroughly defrosted if frozen
1 quantity of stuffing (see page 50)
125 g/4 oz butter
8 rashers streaky bacon
bunches of fresh herbs or watercress to garnish

1 Remove the turkey giblets and use them for making the gravy (see page 53). Wipe the bird with paper towels, and then stuff the neck cavity of the bird loosely with the chosen stuffing. Do not pack it in too tightly, as it expands during cooking. Secure with string or skewers.

2 Place the turkey in a large roasting tin. Rub the butter all over it and cover loosely with foil. Roast in a preheated oven at 220°C/425°F/Gas Mark 7 for 40 minutes; then reduce the oven temperature to 180°C/350°F/Gas Mark 4 and roast for a further 2½–3 hours.

3 To make the bacon rolls, stretch the rashers with the back of a knife and snip each rasher into 2 pieces. Roll up tightly.

4 Remove the turkey from the oven and discard the foil. Baste well. Tuck the bacon rolls around the bird and roast for a further 20–30 minutes, until the turkey is well-browned. Test that the turkey is thoroughly cooked by piercing the thickest part of the flesh with a skewer – the juices should run clear without any trace of pink. Cook for longer, if necessary.

5 Remove the turkey from the oven and allow it to rest for 15–20 minutes before carving. Serve, garnished with fresh herbs or watercress and the bacon rolls.

DEFROSTING TURKEY

Make sure that a frozen turkey is completely defrosted before it is cooked – this is very important. The best way to defrost it is to put it in the refrigerator 2–3 days before Christmas Day, to allow it to defrost slowly. Check the thawing times recommended on the packaging for the size of bird that you have bought.

Avoid stuffing the body cavity of the bird as this can prevent thorough cooking – stuff just the neck cavity.

STEP 1: Meatballs

STEP 2: Meatballs

STEP 1: Stuffing

STEP 2: Stuffing

STUFFINGS

These little forcemeat balls are flavoured with lemon rind and parsley and then rolled in nibbed almonds. When they are roasted, they become deliciously crunchy. Alternatively, you can use the more conventional recipe for Sage & Onion Stuffing given here.

ALMOND & LEMON MEATBALLS

MAKES ABOUT **20**

*30 g/1 oz butter
1 small onion, chopped finely
1 tsp finely grated lemon rind
1 tbsp chopped fresh parsley
1 egg
175 g/6 oz pork sausagemeat
175 g/6 oz fresh white breadcrumbs
125 g/4 oz nibbed almonds
salt and pepper*

1 Melt the butter in a small saucepan and fry the onion gently until softened, about 5–8 minutes. Transfer the onion and butter to a blender or food processor and add the lemon rind, parsley, egg, sausagemeat and breadcrumbs. Season with salt and pepper, and blend for a few seconds to combine. Alternatively, mix all the ingredients together in a large bowl until thoroughly combined.

2 Form the mixture into about 20 small balls. Roll in the nibbed almonds and place around the turkey for the last 30 minutes of cooking time, or roast separately in a small baking dish with 2 tbsp vegetable oil.

SAGE & ONION STUFFING

MAKES ABOUT **500** G/**1** LB

*60 g/2 oz butter
2 large onions, chopped roughly
175 g/6 oz wholemeal breadcrumbs
1 tbsp crumbled dried sage leaves
1 tsp dried thyme
1 egg, beaten
salt and pepper*

1 Melt the butter in a saucepan and fry the onions gently until softened, about 5–8 minutes.

2 Add the breadcrumbs, crumbled sage leaves and thyme. Season well with salt and pepper and mix in the beaten egg. Either use to stuff the turkey before cooking (see page 48) or transfer to a baking dish and bake with the turkey for the last 20 minutes of cooking time.

OTHER STUFFINGS

You can be experimental with stuffing mixtures, adding other herbs or spices to give them different flavours. Try chopped fresh coriander (cilantro) and grated lime rind instead of parsley and lemon.

BREAD SAUCE & TURKEY GRAVY

Make these traditional accompaniments to turkey to serve for Christmas Day lunch. The bread sauce couldn't be simpler to make, and the turkey gravy is very tasty as it's made using the turkey giblets.

STEP 1: Bread Sauce

BREAD SAUCE

SERVES 8–10

1 onion
5–6 cloves
450 ml/³/₄ pint milk
1 small bay leaf
90 g/ 3 oz fresh white breadcrumbs
15 g/¹/₂ oz butter
salt and pepper

1 Stud the onion with the cloves and put into a saucepan with the milk, salt and bay leaf. Heat until almost boiling and then remove from the heat. Allow to infuse for about 20–30 minutes and then remove the bay leaf.

2 Add the breadcrumbs and butter to the saucepan, stirring to mix. Cook gently for 10–15 minutes, stirring occasionally, and then remove the onion and cloves. Season with pepper.

ALTERNATIVES

Make the gravy using the cooking water from vegetables such as carrots and potatoes. Alternatively, use a vegetable stock cube.

TURKEY GRAVY

MAKES ABOUT 600 ML/1 PINT

turkey giblets, rinsed thoroughly
600 ml/ 1 pint vegetable stock
2–3 tsp cornflour, blended with a little cold water
2–3 drops of gravy browning (optional)
salt and pepper

1 Put the turkey giblets into a roasting tin and roast in a preheated oven at 220°C/ 425°F/ Gas Mark 7 for about 30 minutes, until well-browned. Remove from the oven.

2 Remove and discard the giblets. Add the vegetable stock to the roasting tin and cook on the hob, boiling steadily to produce a rich brown colour.

3 Add the blended cornflour to the gravy and cook, stirring constantly, until blended and thickened. Season to taste, adding a few drops of gravy browning, if necessary.

STEP 2: Bread Sauce

STEP 2: Turkey Gravy

STEP 3: Turkey Gravy

STEP 1

STEP 3

STEP 4

STEP 5

CHESTNUT & MUSHROOM CORNETS WITH SHERRY SAUCE

For vegetarians, these cornets of puff pastry – filled with mushrooms, shallots, chestnuts, garlic and herbs – are a special treat. The sherry sauce complements them perfectly.

SERVES 4

500 g/1 lb frozen puff pastry, thawed
1 small egg, beaten
60 g/2 oz butter
2 garlic cloves, crushed
125 g/4 oz shallots, chopped
350 g/12 oz chestnut mushrooms, wiped
  and sliced
125 g/4 oz canned chestnuts, chopped
  roughly
180 ml/6 fl oz medium sherry
1 tbsp chopped fresh parsley
salt and pepper
sprigs of fresh parsley, to garnish

1 Roll out the pastry thinly on a lightly floured work surface and cut into narrow strips. Moisten the edges of the pastry with a little water and use the strips to wind around 8 well-greased cream horn tins. Place them on a greased baking sheet, seam-side underneath. Brush with beaten egg, to glaze.

2 Bake in a preheated oven at 200°C/ 400°F/ Gas Mark 6, until golden brown, about 10–15 minutes.

3 Melt the butter in a large saucepan and add the garlic and shallots. Cook over a low heat for about 15

minutes, until the shallots are very tender.

4 Add the mushrooms and chestnuts to the saucepan and cook over a medium heat for 3–4 minutes. Pour in the sherry and add the parsley. Simmer over a very low heat for 15–20 minutes.

5 Remove the puff pastry cornets carefully from the cream horn tins. Spoon the mushroom mixture into them and arrange on warmed serving plates, allowing 2 per serving. Pour a little sherry sauce around them and serve with fresh vegetables.

VARIATION

Instead of making individual cornets, the puff pastry can be rolled into a large rectangle. Spoon the filling into the middle, dampen the edges of the pastry, fold over and seal. Bake in the oven at 200°C/400°F/Gas Mark 6 for 25–30 minutes, until risen and golden brown.

STEP 1: Potatoes

STEP 2: Potatoes

STEP 1: Carrots

STEP 1: Cabbage

SEASONAL VEGETABLES

These vegetables are to serve with the Christmas Roast Turkey or Chestnut & Mushroom Cornets with Sherry Sauce. Avoid overcooking them on Christmas Day – it's easy to be too eager and start cooking them too early, but in fact they need very little time to prepare and cook.

CRISPY ROAST POTATOES

SERVES 6–8

2 kg/4 lb potatoes
vegetable oil for roasting
salt

1 Peel the potatoes and cut them into large, even-sized chunks. Put them into a large saucepan of cold water with ½ tsp salt. Bring to the boil, and then reduce the heat. Cover and simmer for 8–10 minutes to par-boil them. Drain thoroughly.

2 Heat about 150 ml/¼ pint vegetable oil in a large roasting tin until very hot. Add the potatoes, basting thoroughly. Roast in a preheated oven at 200°C/400°F/Gas Mark 6 for about 1 hour, basting occasionally, until crisp and golden brown.

HONEY-GLAZED CARROTS

SERVES 6–8

1 kg/2 lb carrots
1 tbsp clear honey
30 g/1 oz butter
2 tsp sesame seeds, toasted

1 Put the carrots into a saucepan and barely cover with water. Add the honey and butter. Cook, uncovered, for about 15 minutes, until the liquid has just evaporated and the carrots are glazed. Serve in a hot tureen, sprinkled with toasted sesame seeds.

SPICED WINTER CABBAGE

SERVES 6–8

1 hard white cabbage
2 dessert (eating) apples, peeled, cored and
  chopped
few drops of lemon juice
30 g/1 oz butter
freshly grated nutmeg
salt

1 Shred the cabbage just before cooking it to retain the vitamins. Add the apples and lemon juice, and cook in a small amount of water in a covered saucepan for about 6 minutes. Drain thoroughly. Season with a little salt and add the butter, tossing to melt. Transfer to a hot tureen and sprinkle with freshly grated nutmeg.

STEP 1

STEP 3

STEP 3

STEP 5

RICH CHRISTMAS PUDDINGS

*Grated carrot adds moisture to these miniature Christmas puddings –
ideal for 1–2 servings. Make them in teacups if you don't have dariole
moulds. Being small, they reheat quickly on Christmas Day, either by
steaming or microwaving.*

MAKES 8

125 g/4 oz dark muscovado or molasses
    sugar
250 g/8 oz seedless raisins
250 g/8 oz currants
125 g/4 oz fresh wholemeal breadcrumbs
125 g/4 oz carrots, finely grated
60 g/2 oz ground almonds
grated rind of $1/2$ lemon
2 tbsp lemon juice
$1/2$ tsp ground cinnamon
$1/2$ tsp ground nutmeg
$1/2$ tsp mixed spice
4 tbsp sherry
150 ml/$1/4$ pint stout
2 eggs
1 tbsp butter

1 Put the sugar, raisins, currants,
breadcrumbs, carrots, almonds,
lemon rind and juice, spices, sherry and
stout into large bowl. Mix thoroughly,
then cover and leave in a cool place for
6–8 hours, or overnight, if preferred.

2 Beat the eggs and add to the
mixture, stirring well to combine
thoroughly.

3 Butter 8 150 ml/¼ pint dariole
moulds, small pudding basins or

teacups. Spoon in the pudding mixture,
top each one with a circle of greaseproof
paper and then cover tightly with foil.

4 Steam over simmering water for 3
hours, topping up with boiling
water as necessary. Remove from the
heat and leave to cool.

5 When completely cool, turn out the
puddings and wrap tightly in
greaseproof paper or foil. Wrap in butter
muslin and tie with string.

6 Steam the puddings for 1½–2 hours
on Christmas Day. Serve with
Brandy Butter (see page 77), Sherry
Cream Sauce (see page 78), fromage frais
or fresh cream.

REHEATING
PUDDINGS

Christmas puddings reheat miraculously
in a microwave. Allow 1–1½ minutes on
Full Power for these individual puddings,
allowing them to stand for 2–3 minutes
before serving. Make sure you remove
any foil wrapping before putting them in
the microwave.

STEP 1

STEP 3

STEP 4

STEP 5

FROZEN CITRUS SOUFFLES

These delicious frozen desserts offer a refreshing alternative to Christmas Pudding. If everyone has already eaten enough, the desserts won't be wasted as they can be kept frozen for another day.

SERVES 4

1 tbsp powdered gelatine
6 tbsp very hot water
3 eggs, separated
90 g/ 3 oz caster sugar
finely grated rind and juice of 1 lemon, ½
 lime and ½ orange
150 ml/¼ pint double (thick) cream
125 g/4 oz plain fromage frais
thin lemon, lime and orange slices to
 decorate

1 Tie greaseproof paper collars around 4 individual soufflé or ramekin dishes or around 1 large (15cm/6in diameter) soufflé dish.

2 Sprinkle the powdered gelatine into the very hot (not boiling) water, stirring well to disperse. Leave to stand for 2–3 minutes, stirring occasionally, to give a completely clear liquid. Leave to cool for 10–15 minutes.

3 Meanwhile, whisk the egg yolks and sugar, using a hand-held electric mixer or wire whisk until very pale and light in texture. Add the rind and juice from the fruits, mixing well. Stir in the cooled gelatine liquid, making sure that it is thoroughly incorporated.

4 Whip the cream in a large chilled bowl until it holds its shape. Stir the fromage frais, and then add it to the cream, mixing it in gently. Fold the cream mixture through the citrus mixture, using a large metal spoon. Using a clean whisk, beat the egg whites in a clean bowl until stiff, and then fold them through the other ingredients.

5 Pour the mixture into the prepared dishes, almost to the top of their collars. Allow some room for the mixture to expand on freezing. Transfer the dishes to the freezer and open-freeze for about 2 hours, until frozen.

6 Remove from the freezer 10 minutes before serving. Peel away the paper collars carefully and decorate with the slices of lemon, lime and orange.

TIPS

These desserts can be covered with freezer wrap and frozen for up to 2 months.

CHAPTER FIVE

BOXING DAY SPREAD

✤

Boxing Day fare traditionally consists of an array of cold meats, salads, desserts and drinks. Inevitably, the turkey makes a reappearance! This chapter is designed to add a few delicious dishes to your repertoire of tried and tested favourites, and gives guidance on foolproof methods for making a Glazed Baked Ham and an Old English Trifle that simply *have* to be there.

It's a good idea to have plenty of salads for the buffet, and for dessert a fresh fruit salad too. They are essential for refreshing the palate, and give those who over-indulged the day before a chance to eat a little less and ease the pressure on their waistlines.

One thing about these gatherings is that you want the food to be kept fairly simple, as you will probably still be feeling the aftershocks from Christmas Day. Avoid having to do too much on the day by doing some of the preparations during the weeks before Christmas. Make the meringue base for the Satsuma & Pecan Pavlova and keep it in an airtight tin; prepare the Spinach, Ricotta & Red Pepper Tart and freeze it; make the trifle in the morning, ready for decorating shortly before you serve it. And enlist some help to prepare the Mulled Wine and Winter Fruit Punch – both are easy to make. Have fun!

Opposite: *The dazzling Christmas display outside New York's famous Rockefeller Centre.*

STEP 1

STEP 3

STEP 5

STEP 6

GLAZED BAKED HAM

The method for preparing and cooking this ham is very simple, and because it is partially simmered in water and then finished off in the oven, you get deliciously moist meat with a golden glazed finish. If you are expecting lots of guests, buy a larger joint.

SERVES 12–16

3kg/6lb unsmoked gammon joint
about 36 cloves
3 tbsp clear honey
60 g/2 oz demerara sugar
finely grated rind and juice of 1 orange

TO GARNISH:
orange slices
bay leaves

1 Put the gammon joint in a large bowl and cover it with cold water. Leave it to soak overnight.

2 Drain the water from the gammon and discard it. Place the gammon in a large saucepan and cover it with cold water. Bring to the boil. Reduce the heat and cover the pan. Simmer gently for 3½ hours (30 minutes per 500 g/1 lb plus 30 minutes).

3 Drain off the cooking water and lift the ham on to a large board. Leave to cool for about 20 minutes, and then peel off the skin, leaving a good layer of fat around the ham.

4 Using a sharp knife, score the fat into a diamond pattern and stud with the cloves. Transfer the joint to a large roasting tin.

5 Heat the honey, sugar, and orange rind and juice gently in a small saucepan until the sugar has dissolved.

6 Brush the honey and sugar mixture liberally over the scored joint.

7 Bake in a preheated oven at 200°C/ 400°F/Gas Mark 4 for 20–30 minutes, until golden brown.

8 Serve cold, garnished with orange slices and bay leaves, accompanied by a dish of Cranberry Relish (see page 40) or Cumberland Sauce (see page 42).

SERVING HOT

You can serve this ham hot if you prefer. Just allow it to rest for 10–15 minutes after it comes out of the oven, to make it easier to carve.

STEP 1

STEP 3

STEP 4

STEP 5

SPINACH, RICOTTA & RED (BELL) PEPPER TART

Frozen filo pastry is used to line a flan tin, which is then filled with a combination of spinach, red (bell) peppers, single cream, eggs and Ricotta cheese. Pine kernels are scattered over the top for a nutty taste.

SERVES 6–8

250 g/8 oz frozen filo pastry, thawed
125 g/4 oz butter, melted
350 g/12 oz frozen spinach, thawed
2 eggs
150 ml/¼ pint single (thin) cream
250 g/8 oz Ricotta cheese
1 red (bell) pepper, deseeded and sliced into
    strips
60 g/2 oz pine kernels
salt and pepper

1 Use the sheets of filo pastry to line a 20 cm/8 in flan tin, brushing each layer with melted butter.

2 Put the spinach into a sieve or colander and squeeze out the excess moisture with the back of a spoon or your hand. Form into small balls and arrange in the prepared flan tin.

3 Beat the eggs, cream and Ricotta cheese together until thoroughly blended. Season with salt and pepper and pour over the spinach.

4 Put the remaining butter into a saucepan and sauté the red (bell) pepper strips until softened, about 4–5 minutes. Arrange the strips in the flan.

5 Scatter the pine kernels over the surface and bake in a preheated oven at 190°C/375°F/Gas Mark 5 for 20–25 minutes, until the filling has set and the pastry is golden brown.

ALTERNATIVES

If you're not fond of peppers, substitute mushrooms instead. Add a few sliced sundried tomatoes for extra colour and flavour.

TARTLETS

Individual tartlets look very attractive and are just right for single servings – this recipe makes 6 individual tarts of 10 cm/ 4 in. This recipe makes an ideal dish for vegetarians, although everyone else is sure to enjoy it too.

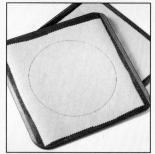

STEP 1

STEP 2

STEP 3

STEP 5

SATSUMA & PECAN PAVLOVA

Make this spectacular dessert for the perfect way to round off a Boxing Day get-together. You can make the meringue base well in advance, ready for filling and decorating just before serving.

SERVES 6–8

4 egg whites
250 g/8 oz light muscovado sugar
300 ml/¹/₂ pint double (thick) or whipping cream
60 g/2 oz pecan nuts
4 satsumas, peeled
1 passion fruit or pomegranate

1 Line 2 baking sheets with non-stick baking parchment or greaseproof paper. Draw a 23 cm/9 in circle on to one of them.

2 Whip the egg whites in a large grease-free bowl until stiff. Add the sugar gradually, continuing to beat until the mixture is very glossy.

3 Pipe or spoon a layer of meringue mixture on to the circle marked on the baking parchment; then pipe large rosettes or place spoonfuls on top of the meringue's outer edge. Pipe any remaining meringue mixture in tiny rosettes on the second baking sheet.

4 Bake in a preheated oven at 140°C/275°F/Gas Mark 1 for 2–3 hours, making sure that the oven is well-ventilated by using a folded tea towel to

keep the door slightly open. Remove from the oven and leave to cool completely. When cold, peel off the baking parchment carefully.

5 Whip the double (thick) or whipping cream in a large chilled bowl until thick. Spoon about one-third into a piping bag, fitted with a star tube. Reserve a few pecan nuts and 1 satsuma for decoration. Chop the remaining nuts and fruit, and fold through the remaining cream gently.

6 Pile on top of the meringue base and decorate with the tiny meringue rosettes, piped cream, segments of satsuma and pecan nuts. Scoop the seeds from the passion fruit or pomegranate with a teaspoon and sprinkle them on top.

MERINGUE

This sort of meringue needs a long time in the oven at a very low temperature to dry it out, rather than cook it – that is why it is a good idea to allow for some ventilation by leaving the oven door very slightly open. Those of you with solid-fuel cookers can leave the meringues in the slow oven overnight to 'dry' out perfectly.

OLD ENGLISH TRIFLE

What would a Boxing Day spread be like without trifle? Follow this simple recipe to produce a delicious traditional trifle that will impress your family and friends.

STEP 1

SERVES 6–8

6 trifle sponges
3 tbsp raspberry jam
150 ml/¼ pint sweet sherry
125 g/4 oz seedless white grapes
125 g/4 oz black grapes, halved and
    deseeded
2 peaches, peeled, stoned and chopped
2 bananas
2 tbsp lemon juice
45 g/1½ oz cornflour
600 ml/1 pint milk
1 tsp vanilla flavouring
3 egg yolks
45 g/1½ oz sugar
300 ml/½ pint double (thick) cream

TO DECORATE:
glacé cherries
angelica
toasted flaked almonds

1 Split the trifle sponges in 2 and spread with the jam. Arrange in the base of an attractive 2 litre/3½ pint serving dish.

2 Sprinkle the sherry over the trifle sponges and spoon in the grapes and peaches. Slice the banana and mix with the lemon juice. Add to the trifle.

3 Blend the cornflour in a large jug with 4 tbsp of the milk. Heat the remaining milk with the vanilla flavouring until warm, and then pour on to the blended cornflour, whisking well. Beat the egg yolks and whisk them into the mixture. Return to the saucepan and heat gently until the mixture is thickened and blended. Remove from the heat and add the sugar. Pour over the fruit and leave to cool completely.

4 Whip the cream until it holds its shape, and then spoon about one-third of it into a piping bag fitted with a star tube. Spread the remaining cream over the custard. Pipe a border of cream around the outside and decorate with glacé cherries, angelica and toasted almonds.

5 Chill until ready to serve.

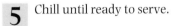

LEFTOVER CAKE

Any leftover plain cake can be used to make trifle – Victoria sandwich cake or Madeira cake is particularly suitable.

STEP 2

STEP 3

STEP 4

STEP 1

STEP 2

STEP 3

STEP 4

MULLED WINE

Make plenty of this warming mulled wine and serve it to your guests as they arrive to give them a glowing welcome. It's the perfect antidote to cold winter weather.

SERVES ABOUT 12

600 ml/1 pint orange juice
300 ml/¹/₂ pint water
3 cinnamon sticks
6 cloves
60 g/2 oz dark muscovado sugar
1 orange
1 lemon
1 litre/1³/₄ pints red wine
300 ml/¹/₂ pint brandy

1 Put the orange juice, water and spices into a large saucepan. Heat gently until almost boiling.

2 Add the sugar and stir until it has dissolved.

3 Using a potato peeler, pare the rind from the orange and lemon. Add it to the saucepan. Slice the orange and lemon thinly and keep covered for using as decoration.

4 Pour in the red wine and brandy, heating very gently until the liquid is very hot, but not boiling. Remove from the heat.

5 Strain the mulled wine and discard the cloves and citrus rind. Keep the cinnamon sticks. Ladle into warmed glasses and serve hot, decorated with the orange and lemon slices and the reserved cinnamon sticks.

SERVING SUGGESTION

Mulled wine makes the perfect drink to serve with warm mince pies and brandy butter. Try the recipes on pages 12 and 77.

ALTERNATIVES

There is no need to use expensive wine in this recipe, so it can be quite economical to make. You could even try making a white wine version, substituting a 1 litre/ 1¾ pint bottle of medium-dry white wine for the red, and using ordinary granulated sugar instead of the muscovado.

STEP 1

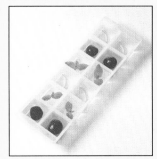

STEP 2

STEP 3

STEP 4

WINTER FRUIT PUNCH

This is a refreshing non-alcoholic fruit punch – ideal for drivers, children and those who prefer not to drink alcohol. It also makes a good pick-me-up on the morning after, for those who have over-indulged!

SERVES ABOUT 12

1 lime
1 kiwi fruit
few maraschino cherries
few mint sprigs
600 ml/ 1 pint English apple juice
600 ml/ 1 pint orange or pineapple juice
1 litre/ 1¾ pints lemonade

TO DECORATE:
1 apple, thinly sliced
1 kiwi fruit, thinly sliced
1 lime, thinly sliced
1 orange, thinly sliced
extra mint sprigs

1 Slice the lime thinly and cut the slices into quarters. Peel the kiwi fruit and cut into small chunks.

2 Put the pieces of lime and kiwi fruit, the maraschino cherries and mint sprigs into ice-cube trays and top up with water. Transfer to the freezer until frozen to use for decoration later.

3 Mix together the apple juice, orange juice or pineapple juice and lemonade in a large glass jug or punch bowl.

4 Decorate the fruit punch with apple, kiwi fruit, lime and orange slices and extra mint sprigs. Ladle into tall glasses and top up with the ice cubes.

ICE CUBES

The decorative ice cubes used in this recipe are very pretty – and so easy to make. Get the children involved in making them – it's just the sort of job that they will enjoy doing.

VARIATIONS

Make your own variations to this delicious drink by varying the types of fruit juice that you use. Substitute peach juice for the apple juice, for instance. Try tonic water instead of lemonade for a less sweet version and remember that if you are trying to watch your weight, you can buy low-calorie lemonade or tonic water to use in the recipe.

PREPARING FOR CHRISTMAS

ROYAL ICING

This recipe for royal icing can be used in place of the fondant icing given on page 12. Royal icing gives a hard consistency.

4 egg whites
1 kg/2 lb icing sugar

1. Sift the icing sugar using a non-metallic sieve.

2. Beat the egg whites lightly in a large bowl and add half the sugar, beating until smooth and glossy. Add the remaining sugar gradually.

3. Spread the icing smoothly over the cake, using a palette knife.

TIPS

Glycerine (glycerol)
If wished, 1 tbsp of glycerine (glycerol) can be beaten in, to give the icing a softer consistency. Glycerine (glycerol) and liquid glucose (used in the fondant icing on page 10) are both available from chemists.

Icing sugar
Sifting icing sugar through a metal sieve can sometimes taint its flavour, so it's preferable to use a plastic one.

THE RUN-UP TO CHRISTMAS

Each year, Christmas seems to come around earlier and earlier. By late September the shops begin to get their stocks of Christmas goods, sending us into a state of mild panic. The actual break itself seems to get longer too, with many people taking up to two weeks off work. Which all adds extra pressure on those doing the preparations, knowing that the catering arrangements for family and friends have extended.

Relax! This step-by-step guide to cooking for Christmas will lead you through the days running up to the festivities and will give you an invaluable source of recipe ideas and information. Whether you've cooked countless Christmas lunches or this is your first time, this book will prove to be a handy reference source, giving you the know-how that's needed to help you survive until the New Year.

TURKEY TIPS

You will probably enjoy the flavour of a fresh turkey more than a frozen bird, but remember to order it in plenty of time from your butcher. Supermarkets also stock a vast number of fresh turkeys during the run up to Christmas, but if you don't have much space in your refrigerator, nor a cold larder or room to keep the bird in, you may have to wait until Christmas Eve to buy it, so make sure that you get to the shops early.

With a frozen bird, you shouldn't have any problems with availability, but you must remember to allow plenty of time for the bird to defrost thoroughly. Check the thawing times on the packaging, and allow up to 2 days for the turkey to thaw properly if it's a large bird. The turkey *must* defrost completely, otherwise the temperature of the bird in the middle does not get hot enough while it cooks, posing a potential health risk.

As soon as you can, remove the giblets from the inside of a frozen bird as it thaws. That way the air can circulate a little more easily and defrosting will be quicker. Refrigerate the giblets and use them for making gravy (see page 53).

COOKING TIMES FOR THE TURKEY

For cooking times, allow the following for different sized birds:

3.5–5 kg/7–10 lb:
30 minutes at 220°C/425°F/Gas Mark 7
3–3½ hours at 180°C/350°F/Gas Mark 4

5–7 kg/10–14 lb:
30 minutes at 220°C/425°F/Gas Mark 7
3½–4 hours at 180°C/350°F/Gas Mark 4

7–10 kg/14–20 lb:
40 minutes at 220°C/425°F/Gas Mark 7
4–5 hours at 180°C/350°F/Gas Mark 7

Do remember that if you have a fan-assisted oven, cooking times will be shortened. You may also wish to reduce the temperature by 10°C/25°F to avoid overcooking.

The best way to test whether the turkey is thoroughly cooked is to pierce the thickest part of the flesh with a skewer. If the juices run clear, then the bird is cooked, but if there is any trace of pink, return it to the oven to cook for longer.

Once the bird is cooked, allow it to rest for about 20 minutes to make carving easier. Keep it wrapped in foil to retain the heat.

COOKING THE GOOSE

If you've decided to have goose for Christmas for a change, make sure that you order well in advance to make sure that one is reserved for you.

Geese range in size from about 3 to 6 kg/6 to 12 lb, but as they do not have quite the same quantity of meat per pound compared to turkey, you may have to order a larger bird. Estimate 350 g/12 oz per person when choosing the weight of the bird.

Cook in the same way as for turkey, but do not butter the bird because it already has a very fatty skin, which eliminates the need. Allow 20 minutes per 500 g/1 lb plus 20 minutes at 190°C/375°F/Gas Mark 5.

Apple sauce is a traditional accompaniment to roast goose, as the sharpness of the fruit complements the flavour of the meat. Apricots also taste good, so add 60–90 g/2–3 oz of chopped dried apricots to one of the stuffing mixtures on page 50 if you are serving goose for Christmas dinner.

CHRISTMAS CAKES AND PUDDINGS

These are the two essentials when it comes to Christmas cooking, so it's very important to get the right recipes to produce the best results. You may have some family favourites that have been passed down from one generation to another, but if not, the two in this book will live up to everyone's expectations.

In both recipes, the dried fruit is soaked for several hours to plump it up and make it full of flavour. This has the added benefit of giving both cake and pudding a more mature taste. If you wish, you can soak the fruit for a much longer period than specified – up to 2 weeks – to give the cake or pudding a truly drunken flavour!

For the alcohol content of the cake, you can use brandy, rum or sherry. And after the cake has cooled completely in the tin, remove it and transfer to a large cake tin, without removing the lining paper. Pierce the top of the Christmas cake several times with a fine skewer and pour two or three tablespoonfuls of brandy, rum or sherry (the same as you used in the cake mixture) slowly over the top. This will help the cake to keep well – and it gives it a bit more oomph! Seal the tin and store the cake for up to 3 months.

The cake can be finished with almond paste and fondant icing (see page 10) or follow the recipe on page 76 for royal icing instead.

Serving Christmas cake
Remember that Christmas cake tastes delicious served with a piece of cheese. Choose from white Stilton or the slightly

This recipe for traditional Brandy Butter uses soft brown sugar in place of the more usual white sugar. The brown sugar gives the Brandy Butter a delicious toffee-like taste and texture that is a real treat at Christmas.

90 g/3 oz light soft brown sugar
90 g/3 oz butter
3 tbsp rum or brandy

1. Beat the sugar and butter together until light and creamy, and then add the rum or brandy, beating well to mix.

2. Transfer to a dish, cover and chill until required. Keep for up to 3 weeks.

3. Alternatively, wrap well in freezer film or foil and freeze until Christmas, allowing a few hours to thaw before use.

SHERRY CREAM SAUCE

This sauce is ideal to eat with
the Rich Christmas Puddings
(see page 58), in place of the
Brandy Butter recipe on page
77.

MAKES ABOUT 450 ML/¾ PINT

30 g/1 oz butter
30 g/1 oz cornflour
300 ml/½ pt milk
150 ml/¼ pt single (thin) cream
2–3 tbsp sweet sherry
about 30 g/1 oz caster sugar

1. Melt the butter in a small
saucepan. Remove from the
heat and add the cornflour,
stirring to mix.

2. Cook over a gentle heat for 1
minute, and then add the milk
gradually, stirring to blend.

3. Add the cream and heat
gently, stirring constantly until
thickened and smooth.

4. Stir in the sherry and reheat
gently, but do not boil. Add the
sugar, according to taste.

5. Serve piping hot with the
Christmas puddings.

TIP

If you wish, add a pinch of
grated nutmeg or ground
cinnamon to the Sherry Cream
Sauce to flavour it.

honey-flavoured Wensleydale – both
complement the rich fruity cake
perfectly.

The Rich Christmas Puddings (see page
58) have a combination of brandy and
stout to give them a deliciously dark and
moist texture. Serve them with a couple
of spoonfuls of fromage frais for a lighter
finish, or make a quantity of Rum or
Brandy Butter or some Sherry Cream
Sauce. The recipes are given on the left
and on page 77 – both taste superb.

USING LEFTOVERS

The golden rule for keeping leftovers of
any description is to cool them quickly
and then cover and refrigerate them.
Never leave them in a warm kitchen for
any length of time – that is a recipe for
disaster. Food poisoning micro-
organisms can multiply very quickly,
making the food unsafe to eat. It won't
necessarily taste 'off', but you could soon
start to feel unwell. So don't spoil the
festivities by being careless with the
leftovers.

Never put warm foods into the
refrigerator – you must allow them to
cool properly first. The reason is that they
raise the temperature of the inside of the
refrigerator, and could possibly bring it
up to the range where the growth of food
spoilage bacteria is not inhibited. And
don't forget to take good care of all foods,
not just the turkey. Wrap them well and
refrigerate, or freeze if appropriate, as
soon as possible.

You may prefer to freeze some of the
leftover turkey, as it's easy to become
bored with it. It's amazing how much

more appetizing it can be in the middle of
January, transformed into a lively stir-fry
with lots of fresh vegetables and spices, or
a satisfying turkey and ham pie, or even
a curry!

PREPARATION AND PLANNING

Whatever you decide to do with the
turkey leftovers, this step-by-step guide
to Christmas cooking will turn the whole
job of catering for your family and friends
over the festive season into a pleasure,
not a chore.

If you are well-prepared for the
Christmas lunch, there is no need to
worry. It is just like making a large
Sunday roast, except you are probably
catering for more people. Turn that to
your advantage – remember, a job
shared is a job halved (forget the one
about too many cooks)! And with any
luck, you might be able to put your feet
up and enjoy a glass of sherry, knowing
that everything is under control. The
most important thing is to enjoy
yourselves!

CHRISTMAS CHECKLIST

To get a grasp of Christmas preparations, it's an excellent idea to write a checklist of things you must buy and do, with a deadline date for certain requirements. It's very easy to forget something, so it makes sense to write things down on a piece of paper and cross them off as you go along. That way you can clear some space in your mind to think of other things. Use the checklist outlined here to give you the basics, and then add your own notes to make sure you have remembered everything.

Early October–late November
- Make the Christmas Cake.
- Prepare the Rum & Raisin Mincemeat.
- Make the mince pies and freeze them.

Late November–early December
- Decorate the Christmas Cake.
- Make the stuffings for the turkey or goose and freeze them.
- Prepare the Rich Christmas Puddings.
- Make the bottled accompaniments to the Christmas dinner – Cumberland Sauce, Cranberry & Red Onion Relish, etc.
- Make food gifts for presents or bazaars.

Early–mid December
- Do any prepare-ahead cooking for parties and buffets, to freeze or store – make the meringue base for the Satsuma & Pecan Pavlova; prepare the Frozen Citrus Soufflés; make the puff pastry horns for the savoury Chestnut & Mushroom Cornets and freeze them.
- Order the turkey if buying a fresh one.
- Buy the turkey if frozen.
- Order extra milk, cream, etc. from the milkman for Christmas.
- Buy the wines, spirits, mixers, etc.
- Shop for all non-perishable foods.

One week before
- Make a list of all the fresh food you need.
- Jot down some reminder notes for things you might forget. (Like the turkey!)

23rd December
- Shop for your fruit and vegetables.
- If cooking a frozen turkey, remove it from the freezer and leave to defrost completely in a cool room.

Christmas Eve
- If cooking a fresh turkey collect it, and any meat that you need, from your butcher.
- Peel the potatoes and put them into water.
- Remove any frozen stuffings and the puff pastry cornets for the vegetarian dish from the freezer. Get some mince pies and brandy butter out too.
- Have a good night's sleep and get up early!

USEFUL TIPS

Kneading dough
When kneading dough, keep your hands lightly floured to make it more manageable and prevent it from sticking to your hands.

Using yeast
There are three types of yeast available: fresh (compressed), dried and easy-blend.

Fresh (compressed) and dried yeast both require mixing with warm water. Fresh (compressed) yeast is usually found in health food shops and is not expensive. Dried yeast can be found in sachets or drums in most supermarkets and chemists.

Easy-blend yeast is very simple to use as it does not require pre-mixing with warm water. It is simply stirred dry into the flour before any liquid is added. It is available in sachet form from most supermarkets.

Chocolate Yule Log (see page 16)
This can be made 2–3 days before Christmas if you keep it in the refrigerator.

INDEX